D0501061

BE BRAVE

An Hachette UK Company
www.hachette.co.uk

Summersdale Publishers Ltd
Part of Octopus Publishing Group Limited
Carmelite House
50 Victoria Embankment
LONDON
EC4Y 0DZ
UK

www.summersdale.com

Printed and bound in China

ISBN: 978-1-78783-232-9

Substantial discounts on bulk quantities of Summersdale books are available to corporations, professional associations and other organisations. For details contact general enquiries: telephone: +44 (0) 1243 771107 or email: enquiries@summersdale.com.

TO..Eletha.......

Love you Sweetie

FROM......................

Mama   Dad
    x o   x o

IF NOT ME, WHO? IF NOT NOW, WHEN?

EMMA WATSON

Life is a
one-time offer
– use it well.

Nothing is impossible. The word itself says "I'm possible".

AUDREY HEPBURN

WHAT YOU THINK
OF YOURSELF IS MUCH
MORE IMPORTANT THAN
WHAT OTHER PEOPLE
THINK OF YOU.

Seneca

If you fell
down yesterday,
stand up today.

H. G. WELLS

TRUST YOURSELF.
YOU KNOW MORE THAN
YOU THINK YOU DO.

Benjamin Spock

BE STUBBORN
ABOUT YOUR
GOALS AND
FLEXIBLE ABOUT
YOUR METHODS.

WHETHER YOU THINK YOU CAN OR THINK YOU CAN'T, YOU ARE RIGHT.

HENRY FORD

Be so good they can't ignore you.

STEVE MARTIN

THE TASK
AHEAD IS NEVER
GREATER THAN
THE STRENGTH
WITHIN YOU.

COURAGE IS VERY
IMPORTANT. LIKE
A MUSCLE, IT IS
STRENGTHENED BY USE.

Ruth Gordon

DO NOT WAIT. THE TIME WILL NEVER BE "JUST RIGHT".

NAPOLEON HILL

The future starts today, not tomorrow.

Imagination is more important than knowledge.

ALBERT EINSTEIN

Self-trust is the
first secret of
success.

RALPH WALDO EMERSON

DO SOMETHING TODAY THAT YOUR FUTURE SELF WILL THANK YOU FOR.

WE ARE A PRODUCT OF NEITHER NATURE NOR NURTURE: WE ARE A PRODUCT OF CHOICE.

STEPHEN R. COVEY

THE MIND IS
EVERYTHING.
WHAT YOU THINK,
YOU BECOME.

Buddhist proverb

THE BEST VIEW
COMES AFTER THE
HARDEST CLIMB.

COURAGE IS NOT SIMPLY ONE OF THE VIRTUES, BUT THE FORM OF EVERY VIRTUE AT THE TESTING POINT.

C. S. LEWIS

You can make
something of
your life. It
just depends on
your drive.

EMINEM

THERE IS NO ELEVATOR TO SUCCESS. YOU HAVE TO TAKE THE STAIRS.

TO FALL IN LOVE
WITH YOURSELF IS
THE FIRST SECRET
TO HAPPINESS.

Robert Morley

A LOT OF PEOPLE ARE
AFRAID TO SAY WHAT
THEY WANT. THAT'S
WHY THEY DON'T GET
WHAT THEY WANT.

MADONNA

Positive thoughts lead to positive results.

With the new day comes new strength and new thoughts.

ELEANOR ROOSEVELT

I'D RATHER REGRET THE
THINGS I'VE DONE THAN
REGRET THE THINGS
I HAVEN'T DONE.

Lucille Ball

HOPE IS THE HEARTBEAT OF THE SOUL.

Always be
yourself. There's
no one better.

SELENA GOMEZ

YOU DON'T GET HARMONY
WHEN EVERYBODY SINGS
THE SAME NOTE.

Anonymous

LIFE IS SO MUCH BRIGHTER WHEN WE FOCUS ON WHAT TRULY MATTERS.

HOW MANY THINGS ARE LOOKED UPON AS QUITE IMPOSSIBLE, UNTIL THEY HAVE BEEN ACTUALLY EFFECTED?

PLINY THE ELDER

Great works are performed not by strength but by perseverance.

SAMUEL JOHNSON

DON'T LIMIT YOUR CHALLENGES. CHALLENGE YOUR LIMITS.

WITH ORDINARY TALENTS,
AND EXTRAORDINARY
PERSEVERANCE, ALL THINGS
ARE ATTAINABLE.

Thomas Fowell Buxton

NOTHING WILL WORK
UNLESS YOU DO.

MAYA ANGELOU

Don't lose your present to your past.

You get in life
what you have the
courage to ask for.

OPRAH WINFREY

Say yes, and
you'll figure it
out afterward.

TINA FEY

WAKE UP WITH
DETERMINATION.
GO TO BED WITH
SATISFACTION.

IN THE END,
EVERYTHING WILL
BE OK. IF IT'S
NOT OK, IT'S NOT
YET THE END.

FERNANDO SABINO

THE KEY TO SUCCESS IS TO START BEFORE YOU'RE READY.

Marie Forleo

NOTHING BUILDS SELF-ESTEEM LIKE ACCOMPLISHMENT.

NEVER GIVE UP ON SOMETHING YOU LOVE.

ARIANA GRANDE

I've learned the main thing in life is you get what you put in.

ADELE

EVEN A JOURNEY OF
A THOUSAND MILES
MUST BEGIN WITH
A SINGLE STEP.

WHEN LIFE PUTS
YOU IN A TOUGH
SITUATION, DON'T
SAY "WHY ME?",
SAY "TRY ME".

Anonymous

AT ANY GIVEN
MOMENT YOU HAVE
THE POWER TO
SAY, "THIS IS NOT
HOW THE STORY IS
GOING TO END."

CHRISTINE MASON MILLER

First dream it, then do it.

Doubt is a killer. You just have to know who you are and what you stand for.

JENNIFER LOPEZ

OPTIMISM IS ESSENTIAL
TO ACHIEVEMENT AND IT
IS ALSO THE FOUNDATION
OF COURAGE.

Nicholas Murray Butler

DIFFICULT DOESN'T MEAN IMPOSSIBLE.

You can do anything if you have enthusiasm.

HENRY FORD

OPTIMISM IS THE
FAITH THAT LEADS TO
ACHIEVEMENT; NOTHING CAN
BE DONE WITHOUT HOPE.

Helen Keller

PUSH YOURSELF, BECAUSE NO ONE ELSE IS GOING TO DO IT FOR YOU.

JUST TRY NEW THINGS. DON'T BE AFRAID. STEP OUT OF YOUR COMFORT ZONES AND SOAR.

MICHELLE OBAMA

Change is hard
at first, messy
in the middle
and so gorgeous
at the end.

ROBIN SHARMA

WHEN
OPPORTUNITY
KNOCKS, OPEN
THE DOOR.

LIFE IS 10 PER CENT WHAT HAPPENS TO ME AND 90 PER CENT HOW I REACT TO IT.

Charles R. Swindoll

THE FUTURE CANNOT
BE PREDICTED, BUT
FUTURES CAN BE
INVENTED.

DENNIS GABOR

You are stronger
than you think.

Life is a helluva
lot more fun if
you say "yes"
rather than "no".

RICHARD BRANSON

There is no way around the hard work. Embrace it.

ROGER FEDERER

BELIEVE YOU
CAN AND YOU'RE
HALFWAY THERE.

IT'S AMAZING WHAT
YOU CAN GET IF YOU
QUIETLY, CLEARLY AND
AUTHORITATIVELY
DEMAND IT.

MERYL STREEP

GREAT SPIRITS
HAVE ALWAYS
ENCOUNTERED
VIOLENT OPPOSITION
FROM MEDIOCRE
MINDS.

Albert Einstein

SELF-CONFIDENCE IS THE BEST OUTFIT. ROCK IT.

SUCCESS IS THE SUM OF SMALL EFFORTS, REPEATED DAY IN, DAY OUT.

ROBERT COLLIER

The only way
to do great
work is to love
what you do.

STEVE JOBS

BELIEVE IN
YOURSELF AND
YOU WILL BE
UNSTOPPABLE.

YOU MUST DO THE
THING YOU THINK
YOU CANNOT DO.

Eleanor Roosevelt

LUCK IS
USUALLY WHERE
OPPORTUNITY MEETS
PREPARATION.

DENZEL WASHINGTON

Persistence is the key to success.

What matters
most is how
well you walk
through the fire.

CHARLES BUKOWSKI

GET OBSESSED, TOTALLY OBSESSED. THERE IS NO USE JUST LIKING WHAT YOU DO. GET OBSESSED WITH IT.

Mario Testino

KNOW YOURSELF TO BETTER YOURSELF.

A head full of
dreams has no
space for fears.

ANONYMOUS

DON'T PRAY FOR AN EASY
LIFE. PRAY FOR THE
STRENGTH TO ENDURE
A DIFFICULT ONE.

Bruce Lee

SMALL CHANGES
EVENTUALLY
ADD UP TO
HUGE RESULTS.

PERSEVERANCE AND SPIRIT HAVE DONE WONDERS IN ALL AGES.

GEORGE WASHINGTON

Do what you can, with what you have, where you are.

THEODORE ROOSEVELT

FOLLOW YOUR
HEART, BUT TAKE
YOUR BRAIN
WITH YOU.

IF YOU CAN DO WHAT YOU
DO BEST AND BE HAPPY,
YOU ARE FURTHER IN LIFE
THAN MOST PEOPLE.

Leonardo DiCaprio

DON'T LET THEM TAME YOU.

ISADORA DUNCAN

Go make it happen.

Never set limits,
go after your
dreams and don't
be afraid to push
the boundaries.

PAULA RADCLIFFE

Knowing what
must be done
does away
with fear.

ROSA PARKS

BE WHO YOU
WANT TO BE. NOT
WHO THEY WANT
YOU TO BE.

YOUR SELF-WORTH
IS DEFINED BY YOU.
YOU DON'T HAVE
TO DEPEND ON
SOMEONE TELLING
YOU WHO YOU ARE.

BEYONCÉ

MY THEORY IS, IF YOU LOOK CONFIDENT, YOU CAN PULL OFF ANYTHING.

Jessica Alba

WE ARE MORE
POWERFUL WHEN
WE EMPOWER
EACH OTHER.

ACT AS IF WHAT YOU DO MAKES A DIFFERENCE. IT DOES.

WILLIAM JAMES

It's the journey, not the end goal, that's important.

EMMA WATSON

SUCCESS DOESN'T COME TO YOU – YOU GO TO IT.

IF YOU WAIT,
ALL THAT HAPPENS
IS THAT YOU GET
OLDER.

Mario Andretti

PERSEVERANCE IS
NOT A LONG RACE;
IT IS MANY SHORT
RACES ONE AFTER
THE OTHER.

WALTER ELLIOT

Stop wishing.
Start doing.

Hard work beats
talent when
talent doesn't
work hard.

TIM NOTKE

THE KEY IS NOT TO WORRY
ABOUT BEING SUCCESSFUL BUT
TO INSTEAD WORK TOWARD
BEING SIGNIFICANT.

Wintley Phipps

MAKE IT HAPPEN. SHOCK THE DOUBTERS.

Those who wish
to sing always
find a song.

SWEDISH PROVERB

I AM TOUGH, AMBITIOUS
AND KNOW EXACTLY
WHAT I WANT. IF THAT
MAKES ME A BITCH, OK.

Madonna

SELF-BELIEF
AND HARD WORK
WILL ALWAYS
PAY OFF.

EFFORT AND COURAGE ARE NOT ENOUGH WITHOUT PURPOSE AND DIRECTION.

JOHN F. KENNEDY

Either you run
the day, or it
runs you.

JIM ROHN

NEVER LET A
STUMBLE IN THE
ROAD BE THE END
OF THE JOURNEY.

SOMETIMES IN LIFE, IT HAS
TO BE ENOUGH TO BE PROUD
OF YOURSELF, EVEN IF NO
ONE ELSE NOTICES.

Duncan Bannatyne

IT'S NOT WHO YOU
ARE THAT HOLDS
YOU BACK, IT'S
WHO YOU THINK
YOU ARE NOT.

DENIS WAITLEY

**Impossible
is just an
opinion.**

Learn how to take criticism. Follow your gut instinct and don't compromise.

SIMON COWELL

Believe in yourself
and be prepared
to work hard.

STELLA McCARTNEY

LIFE IS A GIFT.
NEVER FORGET
TO ENJOY EVERY
MOMENT.

SCAR TISSUE
IS STRONGER
THAN REGULAR
TISSUE. REALIZE
THE STRENGTH,
AND MOVE ON.

HENRY ROLLINS

DON'T TAKE "NO"
FOR AN ANSWER.
NEVER SUBMIT
TO FAILURE.

Winston Churchill

One positive
thought can
change your
whole day.

THE MORE WE DO, THE MORE WE CAN DO.

WILLIAM HAZLITT

Always do what you are afraid to do.

RALPH WALDO EMERSON

IF YOU HAVE
DISCIPLINE AND
DETERMINATION,
NOTHING IS
IMPOSSIBLE.

MY MISSION IN
LIFE IS NOT MERELY
TO SURVIVE, BUT
TO THRIVE.

Maya Angelou

YOUR LIFE IS A
BOOK; MAKE IT
A BESTSELLER.

SHANON GREY

Nothing great ever came that easy.

All successes
begin with
self-discipline.
It starts
with you.

DWAYNE JOHNSON

WHY CHANGE? EVERYONE
HAS HIS OWN STYLE. WHEN
YOU HAVE FOUND IT, YOU
SHOULD STICK TO IT.

Audrey Hepburn

NEVER LET YOUR FEAR DECIDE YOUR FUTURE.

Your time
is limited, so
don't waste it
living someone
else's life.

STEVE JOBS

IF YOU SPEND TOO
MUCH TIME THINKING
ABOUT A THING YOU'LL
NEVER GET IT DONE.

Bruce Lee

**KEEP GOING.
YOU ARE
GETTING
THERE.**

ONCE YOU REPLACE NEGATIVE THOUGHTS WITH POSITIVE ONES, YOU'LL START HAVING POSITIVE RESULTS.

WILLIE NELSON

A wise man
will make more
opportunities
than he finds.

FRANCIS BACON

NO GOAL WAS EVER MET WITHOUT A LITTLE SWEAT.

HAPPINESS DOESN'T
DEPEND UPON WHO YOU
ARE OR WHAT YOU HAVE;
IT DEPENDS SOLELY UPON
WHAT YOU THINK.

Dale Carnegie

ANYONE CAN HIDE.
FACING UP TO
THINGS, WORKING
THROUGH THEM,
THAT'S WHAT MAKES
YOU STRONG.

SARAH DESSEN

Life is too short to be average.

Every moment
is a fresh
beginning.

T. S. ELIOT

You have to believe that something different can happen.

WILL SMITH

DON'T LET
ANYONE SAY YOU
CAN'T DO IT.

HISTORY HAS
SHOWN US THAT
COURAGE CAN BE
CONTAGIOUS AND
HOPE CAN TAKE ON
A LIFE OF ITS OWN.

MICHELLE OBAMA

MOTIVATION GETS YOU GOING AND HABIT GETS YOU THERE.

Zig Ziglar

TREAT YOURSELF
LIKE YOU'RE
SOMEBODY WHO
MATTERS.

YOU'RE ALLOWED
TO SCREAM. YOU'RE
ALLOWED TO CRY. BUT
YOU'RE NOT ALLOWED
TO GIVE UP.

ANONYMOUS

Every limit is
a beginning
as well as an
ending.

GEORGE ELIOT

A BRAVE MIND
CREATES
POSSIBILITIES
AND MAKES
OPPORTUNITIES.

THE FUTURE DEPENDS ON WHAT YOU DO TODAY.

Mahatma Gandhi

IF YOU CAN BELIEVE
IN SOMETHING
GREAT, I FEEL LIKE
YOU CAN ACHIEVE
SOMETHING GREAT.

KATY PERRY

Joy is the ultimate beautifier.

It's OK to say,
"This is what I
want" and go
after it.

ZOE SALDANA

DO NOT SURRENDER TO FATE
AFTER A SINGLE FAILURE.
FAILURE, AT MOST,
PRECEDES SUCCESS.

Sri Chinmoy

LIFE IS SHORT. CHOOSE HAPPINESS.

Courage is found
in unlikely places.

J. R. R. TOLKIEN

THE MOST CERTAIN WAY TO
SUCCEED IS ALWAYS TO TRY
JUST ONE MORE TIME.

Thomas Edison

DREAMS DON'T WORK UNLESS YOU DO.

THERE ARE NO REGRETS IN LIFE, JUST LESSONS.

JENNIFER ANISTON

Who you are
tomorrow begins
with what you
do today.

TIM FARGO

YOU HAVE TO BELIEVE IN
YOURSELF WHEN NO ONE ELSE
DOES. THAT MAKES YOU A
WINNER RIGHT THERE.

Venus Williams

If you're interested in finding out more about our books, find us on Facebook at **Summersdale Publishers** and follow us on Twitter at **@Summersdale**.

www.summersdale.com

Image credits
pp.5, 17, 29, 41, 53, 65, 77, 89, 101,
113, 125, 137, 149, 159 © Alenka
Karabanova/Shutterstock.com